A Little American Cookbook

Kent Dur Russell

ILLUSTRATED BY KAREN BAILEY

First published in 1989 by The Appletree
Press Ltd, 7 James Street South, Belfast
BT2 8DL. Text © Kent Dur Russell,
1989. Illustrations © Karen Bailey,
1989. Editorial consultant: Barbara
Bloch. Printed in Hong Kong. All rights
reserved. No part of this publication may
be reproduced or transmitted in any form
or by any means, electronic or mechanical,
photocopying, recording or any information
and retrieval system, without permission in
writing from the publishers.

First published in the United States in 1989
by Chronicle Books, 275 Fifth Street, San
Francisco, CA 94103
ISBN 0-87701-613-5

9 8 7 6 5 4 3 2

Introduction

Writing a small American cookbook is not easy because America is such a huge country with such a diverse cuisine. Almost the only recipes that can be considered one hundred percent American in origin are those recipes that may have come from American Indians, were developed from ingredients indigenous to America, or have been created by modern-day American chefs. Most other recipes evolved, in one way or another, from the cultural backgrounds of the immigrant population that make up the wonderful melting pot of America. What has made these recipes American is the way they have changed over time to reflect the blending of all the cultures.

A note on measures
Recipes are for four people unless stated otherwise.

Brunch

Sunday breakfast in many American homes is a special occasion. The clever inventors of brunch have found a way to extend the hours to indulge, guilt-free, in the calorific evils of a big breakfast. With typical American ingenuity, breakfast and lunch are combined to create a new meal called brunch . This is a festive occasion for the gathering of friends on a late Sunday morning or early Sunday afternoon. As friends assemble to idle over this wonderful leisurely meal, they are likely to begin with a Bloody Mary (recipe page 56), Screw Driver, or Mimosa (drinks, not tools or flowers).

The three recipes that follow are typical of the kind of food that may be served. The first recipe is somewhat elegant, the other two are simpler, but nonetheless delicious.

Eggs Benedict

This excellent recipe is outrageously delicious. It combines a classic French Hollandaise sauce with typical American breakfast fare.

Hollandaise Sauce	Eggs
6 egg yolks	3 English muffins, split,
2 tbsp cold water	toasted, and buttered
1 cup butter	6 slices sautéed cooked
¼ tsp salt	ham or Canadian bacon
1 tsp lemon juice	6 eggs, poached

salt and black pepper
paprika to garnish
(serves 3)

To make Hollandaise sauce, place egg yolks and water in top of double boiler set over (not in) lightly simmering water (bain-marie). Beat until fluffy. Dice butter and add to egg yolks, a few pieces at a time, beating constantly until butter melts and sauce begins to thicken. Add salt and lemon juice. Set aside and keep warm. (If sauce should curdle, add either very hot water or ice water, 1/2 teaspoon at a time, beating constantly until sauce is reconstituted.)

To serve, place 2 toasted muffin halves, butter side up, on each serving plate. Top with ham and then poached egg. Season with salt and pepper. Spoon Hollandaise sauce over eggs and garnish with paprika.

Pancakes, Griddle Cakes, or Flapjacks

Whether you call them Pancakes, Griddle Cakes, or Flapjacks (all names that apply to the same recipe), they are popular all over America. The best pancakes are served in New England where real maple syrup is easily available to serve with them. Sweet butter, real warm maple syrup (no imitations please), crisp bacon or breakfast sausages, and hot strong coffee are essential accompaniments.

1 cup all-purpose flour	*1 cup milk*
2 tsp baking powder	*1 tbsp melted butter*

¼ tsp salt   butter to grease griddle
1 egg, beaten

Sift dry ingredients into medium-sized bowl. Stir in egg, milk, and butter until well-combined. Pour into pitcher. Lightly grease griddle or skillet with butter and heat until drop of water dances on surface. Pour batter onto griddle in uniform amounts. Cook until surface of pancakes is covered with bubbles. Flip over with wide spatula and cook until lightly browned on second side. Remove to serving plate and keep warm. Repeat with remaining batter, regreasing griddle as necessary. Makes about twelve 3-4 inch pancakes.

Bagels and Lox

Bagels, originally brought to America from Poland, Austria, and Germany are made of raised dough that is shaped, simmered in water, and then baked. They are shaped like doughnuts, with a hole in the middle and are crusty on the outside and very chewy on the inside.

This classic Jewish concoction was originally only found in cities with large Jewish populations, but it has gained popularity all over the United States.

1 bagel (plain, onion, or garlic), split in half and toasted
3 tbsp cream cheese

4 thin slices smoked salmon (lox)
2 slices tomato (optional)
2 slices onion (optional)
capers (optional)

(serves one)

Spread each half bagel with cream cheese and top with 2 slices smoked salmon. If desired add 1 slice tomato, 1 slice onion, and a few capers to each half. Serve as 2 open sandwiches. Do not close.

Sandwiches

American sandwiches range from a very ordinary melted cheese sandwich to the New York specialty Pastrami on Rye or the all-American BLT or triple decker Club Sandwich. A great American sandwich should be very thick.

Pastrami on Rye

This sandwich is a Jewish classic and I am willing to travel great distances to find really good pastrami. As with some of the classic regional recipes found only in certain parts of France, the very best pastrami is only found in New York City in good Jewish delicatessens. It should be lean, cut very thin and treated like precious prosciutto.

---

2 slices pumpernickel or rye bread
mustard
¼ lb warm pastrami
(serves one)

Spread 1 side of each slice of bread with mustard. Place meat between bread slices and cut sandwich in half. Serve with coleslaw and sour garlic pickle.

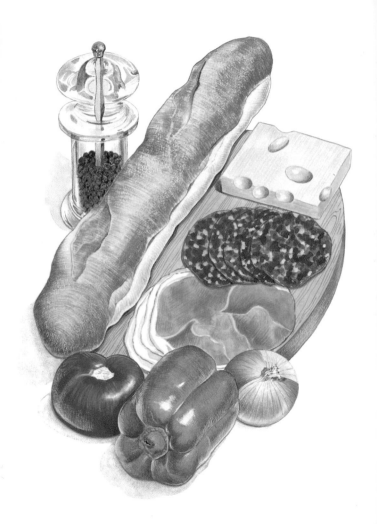

The Heroic Hero Sandwich

What you are likely to call this sandwich depends on what part of the country you are in. In New York it is a Hero; in the South it is a Hoagie or Poor Boy; in New England it is a Submarine or Grinder. The essential ingredients are lots of meat, lots of different kinds of cheese, and salad, arranged on a split loaf of Italian bread. My version is unusual because it is baked, which most Hero sandwiches are not.

1 loaf Italian bread, split in half lengthwise
olive oil for brushing
garlic salt to taste
10 thin slices salami (any kind)
10 slices cheese (provolone, Swiss, Gruyère, or Münster)
10 slices baked ham (any kind)
1 large green pepper, diced
Italian seasoning and freshly ground pepper to taste
1 cup shredded mozzarella cheese
salad for topping: shredded lettuce, sliced tomatoes or onions, coleslaw

Preheat oven to 325°F. Place bread, cut side up, on baking sheet. Brush top of bread with olive oil and sprinkle with garlic salt. Arrange salami, sliced cheese, and ham in layers on both sides of bread. Top with green pepper and sprinkle with seasoning, pepper and shredded cheese. Bake for 15 minutes. Turn off oven and turn on broiler. Broil until lightly browned on top. Cover sandwich with any combination of salad toppings and close it. Cut into 4-inch wedges and serve with ice cold beer.

BLT and Club Sandwich

BLT stands for bacon, lettuce, and tomato. Add some slices of cooked white turkey meat and you have a Club Sandwich. Make the sandwich with three slices of bread and you have a double-decker. Add a fourth slice of bread (and a very wide mouth) and you have a triple-decker.

3 slices white bread, toasted	*6 slices crisp cooked bacon*
mayonnaise or thousand island (Russian) dressing	*4 slices cooked white turkey (Club Sandwich only)*
lettuce	*salt and freshly ground pepper to taste*
4 slices tomato	
(serves one)	

Spread mayonnaise on 1 side of a slice of toast. Cover with lettuce, 2 slices tomato, 3 slices bacon, and 2 slices turkey, if desired. Season with salt and pepper. Spread second slice of toast with mayonnaise on both sides and place on turkey. Cover with lettuce and remaining ingredients. Season with salt and pepper. Spread mayonnaise on 1 side of remaining piece of toast and cover sandwich. Cut into 4 triangles and anchor with fancy toothpicks.

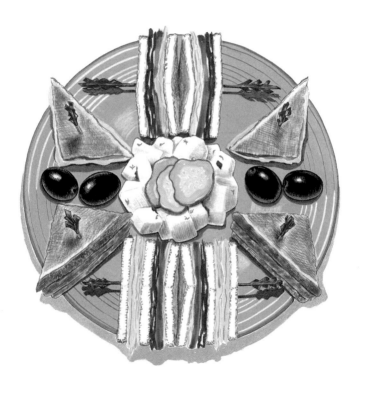

Quick Breads

When a loaf of bread is made with baking powder as the rising agent instead of yeast, it is called a quick bread because the ingredients can be mixed and popped in the oven without waiting for the yeast to cause the dough to rise.

Corn Bread and Corn Muffins

1 cup all-purpose flour	*2 eggs*
1 cup cornmeal	*1 cup milk*
3 tbsp sugar	*¼ cup (½ stick) butter,*
1 tbsp baking powder	*melted*
1 tsp salt	

Preheat oven to 425°F. Grease an 8-inch square baking pan. Stir dry ingredients in large bowl until well-combined. Beat eggs, milk, and melted butter together. Make well in center of dry ingredients and pour milk mixture into it. Stir until dry ingredients are just moistened.

To make Corn Bread, pour batter into prepared pan. Bake 20 to 25 minutes or until top is lightly browned. Cut into squares and serve warm with butter.

To make Corn Muffins, grease 12-cup muffin pan. Fill muffin cups about two-thirds full and bake 15 to 20 minutes or until tops are lightly browned. Remove from pan and serve warm with butter.

Boston Brown Bread

This wonderful regional specialty is traditionally served with Boston Baked Beans (recipe page 27). Serve warm with butter or cream cheese.

1 cup cornmeal	1 tsp salt
1 cup rye flour	2 cups buttermilk
1 cup whole-wheat flour	¾ cup molasses
2 tsp baking soda	1 cup raisins

Thoroughly grease two 1 lb coffee cans and set aside. Stir dry ingredients in large bowl until well-combined. Stir buttermilk into molasses. Make well in center of dry ingredients and pour buttermilk mixture into it. Stir until mixture is blended and dry ingredients are moistened, then add raisins. Spoon batter into coffee cans, filling cans two-thirds full. Cut 2 pieces of aluminum foil large enough to cover tops of cans. Grease foil on 1 side and place, greased side down, over cans. Press foil firmly around sides of cans or secure with string. Place filled cans on rack in large saucepan. Pour in enough boiling water to come halfway up side of cans. Cover saucepan and simmer 1½ to 2 hours or until cake tester, inserted in center of each loaf, comes out clean. Add additional boiling water as necessary during cooking to maintain water level in saucepan. Cool cans upright on wire rack 2 minutes. Remove bread from cans and cool further on rack. Cut into thick slices.

New England Clam Chowder

When I was a child we spent our summers on Long Island digging for clams, and when they were plentiful we would make a chowder. New England Clam Chowder is a favorite throughout the country.

---

12 medium-sized littleneck or cherry stone clams	2 tbsp all-purpose flour
1/4 lb salt pork, finely diced	2 cups milk
1 large onion, chopped	1 cup heavy cream
3 medium-sized peeled, cubed potatoes, cooked	salt and white pepper
	butter to serve (optional)
	chopped fresh parsley

(serves 6-8)

Scrub clams under cold running water. Steam until all clams open (discard any that do not). Strain clam broth and set aside. Shuck (shell) clams, chop, and set aside. Place salt pork in large heavy saucepan and cook over low heat until lightly browned. Add onion and cook until transparent. Discard pork, if desired. Stir in flour and cook 1 minute. Add 3 cups reserved clam broth to saucepan slowly, stirring. Add potatoes, reserved clams, milk, and cream. Season with salt, if necessary, and pepper. Cook over low heat (do not boil) until thickened and heated through. Spoon into small soup bowls and garnish with parsley and pat of butter.

Blackened Salmon Fillets

This Creole recipe was created by Paul Prudhomme, the Louisiana chef. Redfish, pompano, or tilefish can be used instead of salmon. This cooking method creates a lot of smoke. The best, and safest, way is to cook out-of-doors over hot coals. Don't cook indoors unless you have a good exhaust fan, and proceed with caution!

---

1 tbsp paprika   1 tsp onion powder
1 ½ tsp pepper   ½ tsp oregano
1 tsp cayenne   ½ tsp thyme
1 tsp garlic powder   salt to taste
(or about 3 tbsp hot Creole seasoning mix)
1 cup melted, clarified butter
6 salmon fillets, about ½-inch thick
(serves 6)

Thoroughly combine seasoning ingredients. Dip fillets in butter, reserving butter that remains. Sprinkle seasoning mixture on both sides of fillets and pat firmly onto surface. Set coated fillets aside. Place cast iron skillet over very high heat for about 10 minutes or until white ash is visible on the surface. Place fillets in skillet, with about 1 teaspoon of reserved butter on top of each. Cook for about 2 minutes or until underside is charred. Turn and spoon butter on top, and cook until charred on second side, about 2 minutes. Remove to warm serving platter and sprinkle with remaining butter. Serve immediately.

Oysters Rockefeller

Most people probably assume Oysters Rockefeller are so named because someone in the Rockefeller family had something to do with their creation. Not so! Credit for the invention of this dish goes to Antoine's Restaurant in New Orleans. Oysters Rockefeller are truly a symbol of New Orleans cuisine.

---

rock salt
24 oysters, shucked, liquor and ½ of shell reserved
1 cup butter, softened
1 lb fresh spinach, cooked and chopped or 2 packages
(10 oz each) frozen spinach, thawed and squeezed
½ cup finely chopped watercress
½ cup finely chopped shallots
¼ cup freshly chopped parsley
½-¾ tsp cayenne
½ tsp basil ½ tsp marjoram
½ cup Pernod
salt and freshly ground pepper to taste

Preheat oven to 450°F. Spread rock salt in four 9-inch metal pie pans. Place pie pans in oven to heat salt. Place 1 drained oyster in each half shell and set aside. Place remaining ingredients in food processor or blender (in 2 or 3 batches if necessary) and process until thoroughly combined. Spoon into bowl. Shape mixture into 24 patties. Cover each oyster with patty of sauce and arrange filled oyster shells on rock salt. If rock salt is not available, use a shallow baking dish, positioning filled oyster shells carefully so they do not tilt. Bake for 15 minutes or until sauce is bubbly and lightly browned. Cool slightly before serving.

Maryland Crab Cakes

Just about the first thing anyone is likely to eat when they arrive in Maryland are the wonderfully sweet crabs from Chesapeake Bay. Nothing else quite equals them.

1 lb lump crabmeat	1 tsp spicy seafood
1 large egg, beaten	seasoning
1 cup soft breadcrumbs	2 tbsp freshly chopped
1/3 cup mayonnaise	parsley
1 tbsp prepared mustard	2 tbsp butter
1 tsp Worcestershire	2 tbsp vegetable oil
sauce	

(serves 6)

Place crabmeat in medium-sized bowl and remove any shells. Combine egg, breadcrumbs, mayonnaise, mustard, Worcestershire, seafood seasoning, and parsley in separate bowl and mix well. Add to crabmeat and stir gently. Form into 6 patties and place in refrigerator for 1/2 hour to firm. Heat butter and oil in large skillet and fry crab cakes until lightly browned on both sides. Serve with lemon wedges and tartar sauce.

Boston Baked Beans

Homemade Boston Baked Beans bear little resemblance to the kind you buy in a can. Serve with Boston Brown Bread (recipe page 17), or hamburgers (recipe page 36).

---

2 cups / 1 lb dried navy beans, small white beans, or Great Northern beans
1 tsp salt   3 tbsp molasses
3 tbsp brown sugar   1 tbsp dry mustard
¼ cup ketchup (optional)
¼ lb salt pork, rinsed, and slashed
1 onion

Pick over beans and rinse under cold running water. Place in large saucepan. Add salt and 6 cups water. Cover and bring to a boil. Boil 2 minutes, remove from heat, and let stand, covered, for 1 hour. Preheat oven to 350°F. Place brown sugar, molasses, mustard, and ketchup, if desired, in bowl and stir until well-combined. Drain beans, reserving liquid. Place beans in 2½-quart earthenware pot. Add brown sugar mixture and stir well. Pour in reserved cooking liquid to cover beans and stir. Bury salt pork and onion in beans. Cover and bake for 1 hour. Reduce heat to 275°F and bake for 6 hours, stirring periodically and adding water as necessary, to keep beans moist. Bake uncovered during final ½ hour of baking. Discard salt pork, if desired, and onion.

Chicken Gumbo

Gumbos, thought of as soup, but much more like stew, begin with the basic brown roux; include the 'trinity' of both Cajun and Creole cooking, namely diced green pepper, onion, and celery; are highly seasoned; can include almost any kind of meat, fish, or poultry; are thickened with okra; are always served over rice; and blend French, Spanish, Italian and African cooking.

½ cup butter
½ cup vegetable oil
2 chickens (3 lbs each), cut into serving pieces
1 cup butter
1 cup all-purpose flour
2 cups finely diced onions
2 cups finely diced green pepper
2 cups finely diced celery
2-3 cloves garlic, finely minced
3 or 4 medium-sized tomatoes, peeled and chopped
1 lb fresh okra, sliced or 2 packages frozen okra,
thawed and sliced
8-10 cups chicken stock or broth
4 tbsp freshly chopped parsley
2 bay leaves 1 tsp thyme 1 tsp cayenne
hot pepper sauce to taste
salt and freshly ground pepper to taste
(serves 8)

Heat ½ cup butter and oil in large heavy skillet. Add

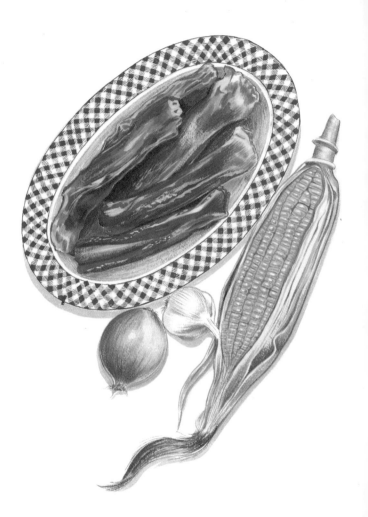

chicken pieces and brown. Remove and set aside. Melt 1 cup butter in large heavy saucepan. Add flour and cook, stirring, until flour is browned. Add onions, green pepper, and celery. Cook over low heat, stirring, about 5 minutes. Stir in garlic, tomatoes with their juice, and okra. Add 8 cups chicken stock slowly, stirring. Add parsley, bay leaves, thyme, cayenne, hot pepper sauce, salt and pepper. Stir well. Add reserved chicken. Cover and simmer ¾-1 hour or until chicken is tender. Add remaining 2 cups stock during cooking, if necessary. Discard bay leaves. Adjust seasoning and serve over hot rice.

Barbecued Spareribs

---

2 tbsp butter
1 onion, chopped
2 cloves garlic, minced
1 cup ketchup
⅓ cup cider vinegar

⅓ cup firmly packed
  brown sugar
¼ cup Worcestershire
  sauce
1 tbsp ginger
hot pepper sauce, salt,
  and pepper
6 lbs pork spareribs

(serves 6)

Melt butter in saucepan. Add onion and cook until almost transparent. Add garlic and cook about 2 minutes. Add remaining ingredients, except ribs, and stir well. Simmer for 20 minutes or until thickened. Remove from heat, cover, and set aside. Divide ribs into serving portions and trim off excess fat. Place in large saucepan, cover with water, cover pan, and simmer about 45 minutes. Drain and pat dry. Brush ribs with barbecue sauce and place over hot grill or in preheated oven at 350°F. Grill or bake for about 30 minutes, turning ribs and basting frequently with sauce. Serve with fresh corn.

Tex-Mex Hot Chili

Chili con Carne, the technical name for this dish, is probably argued about more than any other recipe in America. Whether you use chunks of beef or ground beef, add kidney or pinto beans, or leave them out, you must add as much chili powder as you can tolerate.

---

4 tbsp vegetable oil
2 lbs beef, trimmed and cut into ½-inch cubes
1 large onion, finely chopped
2 cloves garlic, minced
1 can (28 oz) whole peeled tomatoes, chopped
1 can (16 oz) red kidney beans, undrained
2 tbsp chili powder, or to taste
1 tsp cumin
1 tsp crushed jalapeño pepper (optional)
1 tsp oregano
salt and freshly ground pepper to taste
cooked spaghetti or rice to serve

grated sharp Cheddar cheese and finely chopped onion
(serves 8)

Heat oil in large saucepan. Add meat and brown. Add onion and cook until transparent. Drain off fat. Add garlic, tomatoes with their juice, kidney beans, chili powder, cumin, jalapeño pepper, oregano, salt and pepper. Stir well, cover, and simmer 1½ hours or until meat is tender. Adjust seasoning and serve over hot spaghetti or rice. Sprinkle with grated cheese and chopped onion.

Corned Beef Hash

This New England recipe originally developed as a way for the frugal New Englanders to use up the leftovers from a New England Boiled Dinner that includes corned beef, potatoes, and often beets. When beets are added, the name is changed to Red Flannel Hash.

---

3 cups diced, cooked corned beef
2 cups diced, cooked potatoes
1 cup diced, cooked beets (optional)
4 tbsp butter
1 large onion, finely chopped
salt and freshly ground pepper to taste
¼ cup milk or beef broth or half and half
6 poached eggs (optional)
ketchup to serve (optional)
(serves 6)

Combine corned beef, potatoes, and beets in large bowl and mix well. Melt butter in large skillet. Add onion and cook until transparent. Add corned beef mixture to skillet and season. Stir well. Press mixture with spatula to flatten into large 'cake'. Cook over moderate heat until bottom is crusty. Turn mixture over with spatula. Pour milk or beef broth over and cook until crusty on bottom. Spoon onto serving dishes and top each portion with poached egg.

Hamburger

O.K. This is not a joke! A really good hamburger is a wonderful and delicious thing to eat. There are two elements to making a good hamburger – the quality of the meat (it must have enough fat to make the hamburger moist and juicy) as well as the extent to which the meat is handled (handle it as little as possible).

1/3 lb freshly ground chuck or well-marbled top round of beef
salt and freshly ground pepper to taste
hamburger bun or crisp roll, toasted
ketchup, mustard, relish, sliced red onions, sliced tomatoes, and/or barbecue sauce
(serves one)

Place meat in bowl, add salt and pepper, and toss lightly with fork. Form patty. Broil over high heat and serve on warm toasted buns or rolls. Arrange remaining ingredients

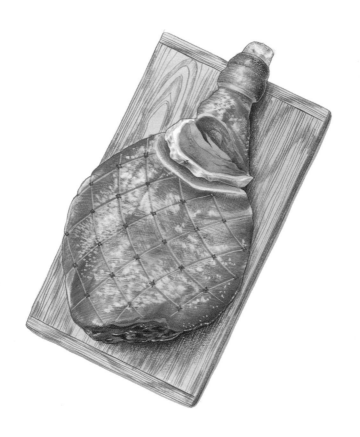

in bowls or plates on serving table and allow people to garnish their hamburgers as desired.

Virginia Ham

Smithfield ham, the famous dry-salted, smoked ham from Virginia, is similar to Westphalian or Parma ham but has its own special and unique flavor. Because of the method used to cure it, it requires long soaking and cooking in water before baking.

---

1 Smithfield or Virginia Country Ham (10-14 lbs)
about 50 whole cloves
Glaze
½ cup honey or light molasses
2 tbsp prepared mustard
1 cup firmly packed brown sugar
(serves 25-30)

Place ham in very large pot or roasting pan and cover with water. Soak for 12 hours, changing water periodically to remove excess salt. Drain ham and scrape off mold. Preheat oven to 300°F. Place ham in large roasting pan. Add 10 cups water and cover pan with aluminum foil. Bake about 20-25 minutes per pound. Remove ham from oven but leave oven on. Remove skin and score it. Stud with cloves. Stir honey, mustard, and brown sugar together and spread over top of ham. Place on rack in roasting pan and bake, uncovered, for 30 minutes. Slice very thin and serve with sweet potatoes and succotash (an American Indian dish made from corn and lima beans). For a special southern touch, baste ham during baking with bourbon.

Salads

Chef's Salad

This salad is never served as a course at a meal, but is a meal in itself. The chef is free to add almost anything he wants to the basic ingredients of lettuce, strips of ham, chicken, Swiss cheese, and wedges of fresh tomato.

---

1 small head iceberg lettuce, finely shredded
1 cup each julienne strips cooked ham,
cooked chicken, Swiss cheese
1-2 medium-size tomatoes, cut into wedges
2 hard-cooked eggs, cut into wedges
salad dressing as desired: vinaigrette, Russian, French,
Italian, or blue cheese dressing
(serves 6)

Arrange lettuce in bottom of six bowls, and scatter ham, chicken, and cheese on top. Arrange tomatoes and eggs on each serving and spoon salad dressing over.

Waldorf Salad

Chef Oscar Tschirky, the famous 'Oscar of the Waldorf' created this salad for a special dinner around the time of the opening of the New York Waldorf Astoria Hotel in March 1893. The basic and classic recipe follows but you can vary this salad in almost any way you choose.

1 cup diced tart apples
1 cup diced celery
½ cup coarsely chopped walnuts
¾ cup mayonnaise
lettuce leaves to serve

Place apples, celery, and walnuts in bowl and mix gently. Add mayonnaise and toss to coat. Cover and place in refrigerator until well-chilled. Arrange lettuce leaves on serving plates and spoon salad onto center of leaves.

Caesar Salad

Depending on what book of food lore you read, Caesar Salad first appeared on a restaurant menu in Mexico City; Tijuana, Mexico; or Baja, California. All books seem to agree the date was about 1920 and its popularity has since spread throughout America.

2 tbsp lemon juice   8 tbsp olive oil
1-2 cloves garlic, finely minced
1 tsp Dijon-style mustard (optional)
6 flat anchovy fillets, drained
1 large head romaine lettuce, torn into bite-sized pieces
1 egg, raw or coddled 1 minute
freshly ground pepper to taste
½ cup grated Parmesan cheese
1 cup freshly made garlic-flavored croutons

Mix lemon juice, garlic, and mustard in large salad bowl. Add olive oil gradually, beating constantly. Add anchovies to bowl, mash well, and stir briskly. Add lettuce and toss gently to coat leaves. Grind pepper over lettuce. Break egg over coated lettuce and toss quickly. Sprinkle with grated cheese and top with croutons

Brownies

Brownies are delicious by themselves or with fruit or ice-cream.

---

2 squares unsweetened chocolate, chopped
½ cup butter   1 cup sugar
2 eggs   1 tsp vanilla   ¼ tsp salt
1 cup sifted all-purpose flour
½ tsp baking powder
1 cup chopped walnuts

Preheat oven to 350°F. Grease 8-inch square baking pan and set aside. Melt chocolate and butter in heavy saucepan over low heat and stir until mixture is smooth. Remove pan from heat and stir in sugar. Let cool. Add eggs and vanilla and stir until blended. Add flour, baking powder, and salt, and stir until well-combined. Stir in walnuts. Pour into prepared pan and smooth top. Bake for 25 minutes. Cool completely in pan set on wire rack. Cut into 2-inch squares.

Chocolate Chip Cookies

Chocolate chips, or bits or morsels as they are sometimes called, are a serendipitous American invention from about 1930.

¾ cup butter, softened
¾ cup firmly packed brown sugar
I egg   I tsp vanilla   ¼ tsp salt
grated rind of I orange
¾ cup all-purpose flour
½ tsp baking soda
I ½ cups rolled oats
I package semi-sweet chocolate chips
(makes about 36 cookies)

Preheat oven to 375°F. Beat butter and brown sugar in medium-sized bowl until light and fluffy. Beat in egg, orange rind, and vanilla. Stir in flour, baking soda, and salt. Add oats and chocolate chips and stir until well mixed. Drop by tablespoonfuls onto ungreased baking sheets about 3 inches apart. Bake for 11-12 minutes or until lightly browned. Cool on baking sheets I minute. Remove from baking sheets and cool completely on wire racks.

Apple Pie à la Mode

Probably nothing sums up old-fashioned American cooking better than the familiar quotation 'As American as Apple Pie.' Serve warm with cheese melted on top or in chunks on the side and ice-cream scooped over it.

I freshly baked double-crust apple pie
I cup shredded Cheddar cheese

Sprinkle Cheddar cheese over top of baked pie. Return pie to oven, 350°F, and bake just until cheese is melted, about 10 minutes.

Pecan Pie

Pecans are native to America, with most of them grown today in the South and Southwest. Pecan Pie is a genuine southern specialty.

3 eggs, lightly beaten
½ cup sugar
1 cup dark corn syrup
¼ cup butter, melted
1 tsp vanilla
1 cup pecan halves
9-inch pie shell, unbaked
ice-cream or flavored whipped cream to serve

Preheat oven to 350°F. Stir eggs, sugar, syrup, melted butter, and vanilla in medium-sized bowl until well-blended. Arrange pecan halves in bottom of pie shell in concentric circles. Pour syrup mixture carefully into pie shell. Bake 50 to 55 minutes or until tip of knife, inserted in center, comes out clean. Cool on wire rack. When ready to serve, reheat and serve warm with vanilla ice-cream or sweetened whipped cream.

Strawberry Shortcake

Traditional Strawberry Shortcake is made with a shortcrust dough formed into two cake layers (or 8 biscuits). However, some prefer it with sponge layers.

Shortcrust Pastry	Filling and Topping
2 cups all-purpose flour	2 lb strawberries
2 tbsp granulated sugar	½ cup granulated sugar
1 tbsp baking powder	1 cup cream
¼ tsp salt	2 tbsp confectioners' sugar
6 tbsp butter	
⅔ cup milk	1 tsp kirsch or vanilla

To make pastry, mix dry ingredients well in a large bowl. Cut butter into small pieces and work into flour mixture with pastry blender or 2 knives until it resembles coarse crumbs.

Make well in center and pour in milk. Mix with fork just until it forms soft dough. Turn out onto lightly floured surface. Flour hands lightly and knead 8 to 10 times. Form into smooth ball and pat evenly in a lightly greased 8-inch cake pan. Bake 15 minutes or until golden in preheated oven at 450°F. Turn out onto wire rack and split in two with serrated knife or 2 forks while still warm. Brush cut surfaces lightly with butter, if desired, and set aside. Wash and hull berries. Reserve some for decoration. Slice the rest and toss with the granulated sugar. Whip cream until almost firm and whip in confectioners' sugar and kirsch.

Spoon half of sliced berries on one cake layer and cover with half of whipped cream. Place second cake layer on top, cut side down. Spread with remaining sliced berries, mound remaining cream on top and decorate with reserved whole berries.

Cheese Cake

The first known Cheese Cake recipe came from ancient Greece, so it can hardly be said that Cheese Cakes are strictly American. However, since cream cheese was developed in America in 1872, Cheese Cakes made with cream cheese are as American as they can be.

Crust
2 cups graham cracker crumbs
¼ cup sugar
1 tsp cinnamon   6 tbsp butter, melted
Filling
1 lb cream cheese, softened
1 cup sugar
4 eggs, separated
grated rind and juice of 1 lemon
¼ cup all-purpose flour
1 cup heavy cream
fresh berries or flavored whipped cream to serve

Preheat oven to 350°F. Grease 9-inch springform pan and set aside. Combine 1½ cups graham cracker crumbs,

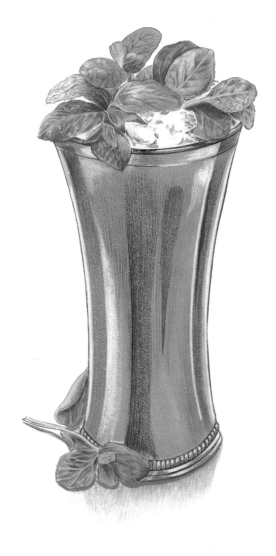

sugar, and cinnamon in small bowl. Stir in melted butter until blended. Press crumb mixture onto bottom and halfway up side of prepared pan. Bake 8-10 minutes. Remove from oven and cool.

To make filling, beat cream cheese and sugar in medium-sized bowl until light and fluffy. Beat in egg yolks, lemon peel, and juice until thoroughly blended. Add flour and cream and beat until blended. Beat egg whites in separate bowl until stiff peaks form. Fold beaten egg whites into cream cheese mixture. Pour into crust-lined pan and smooth top. Sprinkle remaining 1/2 cup of crumbs over top. Bake 1 hour. Cool completely in oven with oven door open. When cool, refrigerate in pan until ready to serve then remove from side of pan carefully and serve cake topped with fresh berries or whipped cream.

Mint Julep

Truly representative of the old South, this is the most famous bourbon drink ever created. If you want to emulate old-fashioned southern aristocracy, serve your Mint Juleps in chilled silver mugs.

---

1 tsp superfine sugar	shaved ice
1 jigger bourbon	mint leaf to garnish
4 sprigs fresh mint	

Mash sugar and mint leaves in bottom of silver mug or old-fashioned glass. Add bourbon and stir. Fill glass with shaved ice and stir until glass is frosted. Garnish.

Bloody Mary · Manhattan

Bloody Mary A popular drink for brunch or lunch.

---

1 tsp Worcestershire sauce or to taste
hot pepper sauce to taste
1 tbsp lemon juice or to taste
salt to taste (optional)
1 jigger/1½ fl oz vodka or gin
chilled tomato juice to taste
freshly ground pepper to taste
lemon wedge and celery or carrot stick to garnish

Place Worcestershire, hot pepper sauce, lemon juice,
salt, and vodka in highball glass. Add tomato juice and
stir. Grind pepper over and garnish.

Manhattan It isn't hard to figure out where this drink
originated. It conjures up a vision of the sophisticated
New Yorker of the 1930s and beyond.

---

1 jigger bourbon or rye whiskey
⅓ jigger sweet or dry vermouth
drop of Angostura Bitters
ice cubes/maraschino cherry to garnish

Pour bourbon, vermouth, and bitters into cocktail
shaker. Add ice cubes and shake well. Strain into
stemmed cocktail glass and garnish with cherry.

Lemonade

3-4 tbsp superfine sugar
I cup water
I ½ tbsp lemon juice (about I lemon)
cracked ice
fresh berries or mint leaf to garnish

Dissolve sugar in water. (Boil 2 minutes, if desired.) Add lemon juice and stir. Pour over cracked ice and garnish with fresh berries or mint leaf.

Ice-Cream Soda

An all-time favorite for children and adults alike.

3 tbsp syrup (chocolate, coffee, caramel, or fruit-flavored)
2 scoops ice-cream (any flavour)
I cup chilled carbonated water
whipped cream and maraschino cherry to garnish

Pour syrup into tall glass. Add ice-cream and carbonated water. Stir gently and top with whipped cream and cherry. Serve with straw and iced teaspoon.

Index